The Best of Mexican Cooking

Recipes from Mexico
and the American Southwest

by Jane Butel

BARRON'S
New York • London • Toronto • Sydney

All inquiries should be addressed to:

Barron's Educational Series, Inc.
250 Wireless Boulevard
Hauppauge, New York 11788

International Standard Book
No. 0-8120-5589-6
Library of Congress Catalog Card
No. 84-9203

**Library of Congress Cataloging in Publication
Data**
Butel, Jane.
    The best of Mexican cooking.

    Includes index.
    1. Cookery, Mexican.   2. Cookery, American—
Southwestern States.   I. Title.
TX716.M4B87   1984   641.5972   84-9203
ISBN 0-8120-5589-6

PRINTED IN HONG KONG
7   490   9 8 7 6 5 4 3

Credits

Photography
Color photographs: Matthew Klein
Food styling: Andrea Swenson
Stylist: Linda Cheverton
Accessories: Mexican ceramics and glassware from
    Pan American Phoenix, New York City;
    stainless-steel flatware from Goerg Jenson, New
    York City; china from D. F. Sanders, New York
    City; flowers by Ann Titus.

Author   Jane Butel is the founder and president
of Pecos Valley Spice Company. Author of seven
books on Southwestern regional cooking, she
also conducts a New Mexican/Tex-Mex Cooking
School in Santa Fe, New Mexico, and in various
department and gourmet/speciality cooking
stores. Frequently appearing on television and
radio and authoring magazine and newspaper
stories, she is considered the leading authority
of this type of cooking.

Cover and book design   Milton Glaser, Inc.

Series editor   Carole Berglie

INTRODUCTION

Southwestern regional cookery is fun . . . easy . . . spicy, and just as exciting as a bright sunny day! And, no wonder—it hails from the land of brilliant sapphire skies, harsh mesas, and terra-cotta landscapes. The cuisine reflects a simple, rugged spirit.

The vast popularity of these spicy dishes attests to the cuisine's pleasures all aficionados share. I believe that, once sampled, well-prepared Mexican-inspired dishes are never forgotten. And then the craving starts! Once you have fresh, clear-tasting chile on your palate, the passion begins! You will be driven to increasingly indulge yourself with cooking and eating these Spanish-inspired, Pueblo Indian dishes adapted by us "Gringos." In plain language, you'll experience the pleasures of a "chile fix."

The basis for these dishes is simple, owing originally to a limited access to ingredients and equipment. Lime-treated corn, lava wheel ground, is the basis for tortillas which, when lightly fried and sauced, become enchiladas. When crispy fried, they become taco shells, tostados, or tostada chips. When added to generously beaten lard, tamales are born. Wheat is a more recent Spanish introduction to the cuisine, and more *au courant* dishes have been created with it, especially tortillas, cookies, and pastries.

Chiles—mostly the developed varieties that average six or more inches long and are bright green or allowed to ripen to a bold red—provide the personality for most of these dishes. The chiles can be made into raw salsas (sauces) for flavoring meats or vegetables and for use as a table sauce. Or they can be cooked into simple red or green sauces with or without meats to accompany enchiladas, tamales, and many, many more of the cuisine's creative dishes.

Besides being a flavoring or the basis for a sauce, chile is a natural preservative, discovered by the Indians. Its earliest known use was for sprinkling on "jerked" meat before drying it, creating jerky. When reconstituted or boiled in water, this jerky was probably the origin of chile con carne, and the world's first convenience food!

Any dish containing chile will retain its freshness for a long period of time. For example, frozen chile-laden dishes will, as a rule, still be quite flavorful even when stored for up to a year—over twice the life of foods not containing an abundance of chile. Tortillas, on the other hand, should not be kept for an extended period of time. Maximum frozen storage is three months.

Simple equipment is all that's required for making Mexican food. The only exceptions are a tortilla press, a heavy griddle or *comal* for baking tortillas, and a thermostatically controlled deep-fat fryer (with a fry basket) for frying sopaipillas, steaming tamales, and stewing chiles. The hard-to-find, elusive tips, techniques, and foolproof hints for making specialties such as tortillas, sopaipillas, tamales, chiles, and the like are carefully explained here. Once mastered, the cuisine's pleasures will be yours forever! ENJOY!

THE RECIPE ANALYSES

For each recipe in this book, you'll note that we have provided data on the quantities of protein, fat, sodium, carbohydrates, and potassium, as well as the number of calories (kcal) per serving. It is recommended for these recipes that you use pure ground chile, available from Pecos Valley Spice Company. Pure ground chile contains no salt or chemicals or additives. Whereas all other commer-

cially available chile powders are 40 percent salt and 20 percent chemicals, additives, and preservatives. Analyses for these recipes are based on pure chile powder and other pure ingredients. If you are on a low-calorie diet or are watching your intake of sodium, these figures should
help you gauge your eating habits and help you balance your meals. Bear in mind, however, that the calculations are fundamentally estimates, and are to be followed only in a very general way.

The following are some basic recipes you'll use over and over as you prepare the dishes in this book.

GUACAMOLE

YIELD

4 to 6 servings

Per serving (4)
calories 172, protein 2 g,
fat 15 g, sodium 280 mg,
carbohydrates 10 g,
potassium 667 mg

TIME

10 minutes preparation

INGREDIENTS

2 ripe avocados
1/2 fresh tomato, finely chopped
2 teaspoons lime or lemon juice
2 green onions, chopped
1 clove fresh garlic, minced
1/2 teaspoon salt
1 fresh jalapeño pepper, finely minced

Halve the avocados, and scoop out flesh into a 1-quart bowl. Cut with a knife and a fork into 1/2-inch cubes. Add remaining ingredients, adding lime juice to taste a little at a time, and stir together.

NOTE For the freshest flavor, prepare just before eating. Salsa Fresca (see below) may be added to taste instead of the tomato, green onion, and jalapeño pepper.

SALSA FRESCA

YIELD

About 1 pint

Per serving (6)
calories 34, protein 1 g,
sodium 4 mg,
carbohydrates 8 g,
potassium 107 mg

TIME

15 minutes preparation
15 minutes marinating

INGREDIENTS

1 large fresh tomato
1 medium Bermuda onion or 2 green
   onions, tops included
1 clove fresh garlic
4 fresh or frozen peeled green chiles
   (see parching instructions in NOTE,
   Recipe 21), or 1 can (4 ounces)
   chopped green chiles
Salt to taste (optional)

Chop tomato, onion, and garlic very fine.

Stir in chiles and salt and allow to marinate at least 15 minutes.

NOTE Salsa Fresca keeps for up 1 week when refrigerated in a tightly closed container. Or, it can be frozen for later use in cooked sauces.

RED CHILE SAUCE

YIELD

1 pint

Per serving (6)
calories 70, protein 2 g,
fat 5 g, sodium 262 mg,
carbohydrates 4 g,
potassium 123 mg

TIME

2 minutes preparation
10 to 20 minutes cooking

INGREDIENTS

2 tablespoons lard
2 tablespoons flour
1 clove garlic
¼ cup pure red chile, mild or hot or
   combination
2 cups beef broth
Pinch of oregano and ground cumino
   (cumin)

Melt lard in a saucepan placed over low heat. Add the flour and garlic and stir until well mixed. Cook until lightly browned. Remove from heat and add the chile. Add the beef broth and mix into a paste, stirring constantly. Continue to cook and stir until a smooth sauce is obtained. Season to taste, then simmer for at least 10 minutes.

VARIATIONS Brown 1 pound ground beef, cubed beef, or ground pork and add to sauce or prepare sauce in pan with meat (omit lard). If preferred, cook chopped onion in fat before adding flour. (Omit raw onion when preparing enchiladas, Recipe 11.)

YIELD

2 servings

Per serving
calories 285,
sodium 538 mg,
carbohydrates 13 g,
potassium 44 mg

TIME

5 minutes preparation
1 hour to frost glasses
    (optional)

INGREDIENTS

3 limes
Kosher or coarse salt
2 ounces (¼ cup) Cointreau
    or Triple Sec
6 ounces (¾ cup) tequila, white or
    gold
1 egg white (optional)

Roll 2 of the limes on a hard surface to fully develop their juice ①. Halve and juice; you should have 2 ounces (¼ cup). Cut remaining lime in half.

Prepare salt-rimmed glasses by pressing lime half around the rim of each glass ②, then dip rims in a saucer of salt ③. Chill glasses in freezer for about an hour if time allows.

Add the lime juice, Cointreau or Triple Sec, and tequila to a blender jar along with 2 to 3 ice cubes. Blend until slushy. If an electric blender is unavailable, use crushed ice and place in a shaker with juice and liquor or vigorously stir in a pitcher.

If a frothy margarita is desired, add the egg white and blend a few more seconds. Serve in salt-rimmed glasses.

NOTE Leftover margaritas can be frozen for 1 month.

2

YIELD

24 tostadas

Per nacho
calories 112, protein 6 g,
fat 7 g, sodium 230 mg,
carbohydrates 7 g,
potassium 70 mg

TIME

30 minutes preparation
5 minutes cooking

INGREDIENTS

1 small package (6 ounces) tostadas
24 ¼-inch-thick squares monterey jack, or 2 cups coarsely grated mixture of monterey jack and cheddar cheeses
24 slices jalapeño peppers, or to taste
Guacamole (optional; see Introduction)
2 cups refried pinto beans (optional; see Recipe 5), heated
Sour cream (optional)

1 tomato, chopped
Pitted black olives (optional)
1 pound chorizo sausage, fried, drained, and crumbled, or 2 cups speedy Chile con Carne (Recipe 23)

Place tostadas on a large, ovenproof platter. Evenly distribute cheese over top and sprinkle with jalapeño slices to taste ①.

Place tostadas under broiler until cheese melts. Then place guacamole in center of nachos ②, put a scoop of refried beans at either end ③, garnish with sour cream and a few sprinkles of extra cheese. Scatter chopped tomato over top of guacamole. Sprinkle olives over tostadas and encircle dish with chorizo or chile.

YIELD

2 cups

Per cup
calories 1718, protein 68 g,
fat 135 g, sodium 3488 mg,
carbohydrates 61 g,
potassium 941 mg

TIME

10 minutes preparation
10 minutes cooking

INGREDIENTS

⅓ cup vegetable oil
½ cup finely chopped onion; or
   3 scallions with tops, chopped
I clove garlic, finely minced
I tablespoon flour
I can (5½ ounces) evaporated milk
I fresh medium tomato, chopped
I pound processed cheese, cut in
   I-inch cubes
½ cup cubed monterey jack cheese

3 tablespoons finely minced jalapeño
   peppers (and juice, to taste)
I package (6 ounces) tostadas

Heat oil in a heavy saucepan. Add onion and garlic and sauté until onion is translucent, about 3 to 5 minutes ①. Stir in flour ②. Remove from heat.

Slowly add evaporated milk ③ and remaining ingredients. Cook and stir until thick and smooth, about 5 minutes. Serve warm with tostadas.

NOTE Keep Chile Con Queso warm in a chafing dish if serving at a party. Leftover Chile is excellent spooned over tostadas for instant nachos, served over hamburgers, or used in omelettes.

4

YIELD

4 servings (3½ cups)

Per serving
calories 619, protein 26 g,
fat 26 g, sodium 818 mg,
carbohydrates 73 g,
potassium 1138 mg

TIME

Overnight soaking
3 hours cooking

INGREDIENTS

2 cups (1 pound) dried pinto beans
5 cups water, approximately
1 large clove garlic, minced
1½ teaspoons salt
¼ cup chopped Spanish onion
¼ cup bacon drippings, or ½ cup
    cubed salt pork
1 small ham hock or bacon rind, or ¼
    cup lard

Rinse ① and sort beans ②; cover with water ③ and soak overnight.

Drain beans and place in saucepan. Add 5 cups water, bring to a boil, reduce heat, and add the garlic, salt, onion, and bacon drippings and ham hock. Simmer until tender, about 2½ to 3 hours, adding more water as necessary. Taste and adjust seasonings. The beans should be very soft.

YIELD

6 to 8 servings

Per serving (6)
(without peppers)
calories 590, protein 25 g,
fat 30 g, sodium 822 mg,
carbohydrates 57 g,
potassium 894 mg

TIME

10 minutes preparation
20 minutes cooking

INGREDIENTS

2 tablespoons lard
2 cloves garlic, finely minced
2 tablespoons finely chopped onion
4 cups cooked pinto beans with liquid
   (Recipe 4), or use canned if you
   haven't time to cook dried beans
Salt to taste
1 cup grated combined monterey jack
   and cheddar cheese

2 pickled jalapeño peppers, finely
   chopped (optional)

Heat the lard in a heavy skillet over medium heat. Add the garlic and onion, and cook until onion is translucent ①.

Add beans to skillet along with a little of the cooking or canning ② liquid and mash them well ③. Add salt to taste. Fry beans over medium heat for about 15 minutes, turning to prevent burning, until a crispy crust forms on edges.

Top with grated cheese and stir in. Sprinkle with jalapeños and serve piping hot.

YIELD

4 servings

Per serving
calories 274, protein 6 g,
fat 8 g, sodium 476 mg,
carbohydrates 42 g,
potassium 297 mg

TIME

5 minutes preparation
25 minutes cooking

INGREDIENTS

1 cup raw long-grain white rice
2 tablespoons lard
¼ cup chopped onion
1 clove garlic, minced
2 cups chicken broth
1 cup peeled and chopped tomato
Salt to taste

Rinse the rice twice in cold water ①. Drain thoroughly.

In a heavy skillet, heat the lard and sauté the onion and garlic until onion is golden. Remove to a plate. In the same skillet, sauté the raw rice until golden ②.

Return the onion and garlic mixture to the pan with the browned rice. Add the chicken broth, tomato, and salt ③. Bring to a boil, reduce heat to very low, cover, and simmer for 20 minutes without lifting the lid. Serve hot.

VARIATION Along with liquid, add a finely minced jalapeño pepper or ground red chile (hot or mild) to taste.

YIELD

12 6-inch, 16 5-inch, 24
   4-inch, or 40 3-inch
   tortillas

Per tortilla (6-inch)
calories 82, protein 2 g,
carbohydrates 17 g,
potassium 27 mg

TIME

10 minutes preparation
1 hour resting
20 minutes cooking

INGREDIENTS

2 cups masa harina
1 teaspoon salt or to taste (optional)
½ to 1¼ cups hot water

Combine the masa and salt, if adding, and make a well in the center of the mixture. Add ½ cup of the hot water and mix in well. Continue adding water a little at a time, mixing well, until a firm dough is formed. Finish the mixing with your hands; this will give you the best dough. It should be firm and springy to the touch, not dry, crumbly, or sticky. If dough is too moist, add more masa; if too dry, add more water. Cover and let rest for 1 hour.

Preheat a *comal* or well-seasoned skillet until very hot. Divide the dough into balls; the size of the balls will vary, depending on the size tortilla you want. Place a ball of dough between lightly moistened sheets of waxed paper or plastic wrap ①, and flatten in a tortilla press, with a rolling pin ②, or with the bottom of a cast-iron pan. Trim the edges, if you wish, to get a nice shape ③. Continue to form remaining tortillas. (At this point, the tortillas may be frozen, stacked with the liner papers between them, and the stacks placed in plastic bags.) Place a tortilla on the hot, ungreased cooking surface and cook for a minute or two on each side. Remove from skillet or *comal* and stack as you cook remaining tortillas; wrap in a warm towel or napkin until you have cooked all the tortillas.

NOTE To make blue cornmeal tortillas, you must use blue corn masa for the masa harina, available by mail order from Sources (see list, Index).

YIELD

6 servings

Per serving (without Salsa Fresca)
calories 588, protein 33 g, fat 35 g, sodium 787 mg, carbohydrates 37 g, potassium 600 mg

TIME

30 minutes preparation
30 minutes cooking

INGREDIENTS

1 recipe beef or chicken taco filling (Recipe 15 or 16) or red chile (Recipe 22)
2 cups Frijoles Refritos (Recipe 5)
6 Corn Tortillas (Recipe 7), crisp fried (left flat or formed into cup; see Note)
6 ounces monterey jack cheese, cut in strips
1 medium avocado, sliced into thin strips
1 cup shredded sharp cheddar cheese
Salsa Fresca (see Introduction)

SALAD MIXTURE

6 rings of a Spanish onion
12 pitted ripe olives, sliced
2 cups torn lettuce, any type (preferably a combination of romaine & iceberg)
1 tomato, cut into thin wedges
Salt

Preheat oven to 350 degrees. Prepare the taco filling and the beans, then place the beans in a layer on each tortilla. Top with the monterey jack cheese. Cover the cheese with warm taco filling and place tostados in oven to heat for 30 minutes.

Meanwhile, prepare salad mixture. Combine ingredients. Lightly salt and spoon on top of tostados.

To serve, garnish the tostado with the avocado wedges, shredded cheese, and Salsa Fresca.

NOTE Restaurants frequently serve these with the bottom tortilla formed into a cup. To shape tortillas, use a pointed can opener to puncture an empty beer can in 4 places along the bottom sides of the can. Then stagger 4 more punctures on the flat bottom of the can. Heat 2 quarts cooking oil in a deep-fryer or 5-quart saucepan to 375 degrees. Float a tortilla, first-baked or lined side up, and immediately center the punctured can on top ①. Using 2 pairs of tongs, press the can into the oil until the tortilla folds up around it as it fries ②. Leave the can and tortilla submerged for no more than 20 to 25 seconds—you will feel the tortilla harden around the can. Lift can from the oil, pouring off excess oil, and gently pull off the tostado shell ③. Drain on paper toweling. When using cup-shaped shells for tostados, serve 2 per person, since they will not hold as much as a flat tostado.

YIELD

9 to 12 servings

Per serving (9)
(without bacon)

calories 317, protein 8 g,
fat 24 g, sodium 480 mg,
càrbohydrates 20 g,
potassium 162 mg

TIME

5 minutes preparation
30 to 40 minutes baking

INGREDIENTS

1 cup blue cornmeal
1 ½ teaspoons baking powder
¾ teaspoon salt
2 eggs
⅔ cup butter, melted, or bacon
   drippings
1 cup sour cream
1 can (16 ounces) or 2 cups whole
   kernel corn
¼ pound monterey jack or cheddar
   cheese, sliced

¼ cup sliced jalapeño peppers
½ cup bacon bits (optional)

Preheat oven to 375 degrees. Grease a 9-inch square pan or 10-inch cast-iron skillet.

Mix dry ingredients and make a well in the center ①. Add eggs, melted butter, and sour cream ②; blend thoroughly. Fold in corn kernels.

Pour half the batter into the prepared pan ③. Cover with sliced cheese and jalapeños. Pour remaining batter over top. Add bacon bits, if desired. Bake for 30 to 40 minutes, or until top springs back when gently pressed with a finger. Serve in squares or wedges with a Bowl of Red (Recipe 22) with fixin's and mixin's listed at end of recipe.

YIELD

2 dozen medium

Per sopaipilla
calories 66, protein 1 g,
fat 3 g, sodium 80 mg,
carbohydrates 8 g,
potassium 22 mg

TIME

10 minutes preparation
10 minutes resting
25 minutes cooking

INGREDIENTS

2 cups unbleached all-purpose flour
¾ teaspoon salt
½ teaspoon baking powder
1½ teaspoons lard
½ package active dry yeast (optional)
¼ cup warm water
½ to ¾ cup scalded milk, cooled to
    room temperature
Oil for deep-frying

Combine dry ingredients and cut in shortening. Make a well in center. Dissolve yeast in warm water. Add to ½ cup cooled scalded milk. (If not using yeast, use ¾ cup milk; recipe works well without yeast, too.) Add liquid to middle of dry ingredients and work into dough, adding only enough additional milk to make a firm dough. Knead dough 15 to 20 times and set aside for approximately 10 minutes.

Roll dough to ¼-inch thickness or slightly thinner, then cut in squares or triangles ①—do not reroll any of the dough. Cover the cut dough with a towel.

Heat oil in a deep-fryer or deep, heavy pot. Bring to temperature of 420 degrees. Add a few sopaipillas to oil at a time ②. They should puff very soon after being dropped in the hot fat. (Hold each down in fat with tongs to assure puffing.) Fry until golden on both sides. Drain sopaipillas on absorbent toweling ③ and serve as a bread with any Southwestern meal. They are especially good torn open and drizzled with honey.

NOTE Sopaipillas may be dusted with cinnamon sugar and served as a dessert with New Mexican chocolate. Or stuff hot sopaipillas with Frijoles Refritos (Recipe 5), Chile con Carne (Recipe 23), and chopped onion and grated cheese for a snack.

YIELD

2 servings

Per serving (without eggs or lettuce)
calories 950, protein 50 g, fat 54 g, sodium 898 mg, carbohydrates 66 g, potassium 746 mg

TIME

10 minutes preparation
10 minutes cooking

INGREDIENTS

6 regular or blue Corn Tortillas (Recipe 7)

Oil

2 cups Red Chile Sauce, with any type of meat added (see Introduction)

I cup grated monterey jack or cheddar cheese, or more to suit taste

I onion, chopped (may be cooked into the sauce)

2 eggs, lightly fried (optional)
6 to 8 leaves lettuce, chopped (optional)

Lightly fry the tortillas in shallow oil in a skillet over medium heat ①, then drain each on absorbent toweling. (For fewer calories, place the tortillas on dinner plates and cover with foil; place in a moderate oven until they are warm and soft.)

FOR FLAT ENCHILADAS Place a little chile sauce on the plate ②, then top with a tortilla ③ followed by cheese, onion, more sauce and meat from sauce if added. Repeat twice more. Top each enchilada with more sauce and cheese. Heat in a moderate oven until the cheese melts. Top with an egg if desired, and garnish with chopped lettuce. These are traditional Santa Fe style.

FOR ROLLED ENCHILADAS Dip the lightly fried tortilla into the sauce and place a strip each of grated cheese and chopped onion down the center. Add a strip of cooked meat from sauce if desired. Roll and top with more sauce and cheese. To serve a crowd, place the rolled enchiladas in a large, shallow baking dish but do not cover with sauce. Just before serving, heat in moderate oven. Warm the sauce separately and add just as you are ready to serve. Do not overcook or the enchiladas will be very mushy. Top with additional cheese and reheat until it melts. Add lettuce around edges before serving.

ENCHILADAS SUISAS

YIELD

4 to 6 servings

Per serving (4) (without olives and tomatoes)
calories 1044, protein 48 g, fat 62 g, sodium 1189 mg, carbohydrates 73 g, potassium 1020 mg

TIME

40 minutes preparation
15 minutes cooking
20 minutes baking

INGREDIENTS

12 Corn Tortillas (Recipe 7)
Vegetable oil for frying
1 cup grated monterey jack cheese
1 cup grated mild cheddar cheese
2 cups shredded cooked chicken or pork
1 cup heavy cream
¼ cup chopped scallions, tops included
Stuffed green olives, sliced
Cherry tomatoes

SALSA VERDE
(Green Chile Sauce)

2 tablespoons butter
⅔ cup chopped Spanish onion
2 tablespoons flour
1½ cups chicken broth
1 cup (or more) chopped green chiles, freshly parched and peeled (Recipe 21) or canned
1 large clove garlic, finely minced
¾ teaspoon salt
Dash of ground cumino (cumin)

Prepare Salsa Verde. Melt the butter in a saucepan over medium heat. Sauté the onion until soft. Stir in the flour. Add the broth. Then add chiles, garlic, salt, and *cumino*. Simmer about 15 minutes to blend flavors, then set aside. Preheat oven to 350 degrees.

In a heavy skillet, lightly fry the tortillas in shallow oil, being careful not to make them too crisp to roll. Combine the cheeses and set ½ cup aside for topping. Dip each tortilla in Salsa Verde (both sides). Place 2 heaping tablespoons chicken or pork and about 2 tablespoons cheese down the center of each ①; roll and place seam side down in a shallow baking dish ②.

After all the rolled tortillas are in the dish, spoon additional Salsa Verde over them, and then cover evenly with heavy cream ③. Sprinkle with remaining ½ cup cheese and with the scallions, and bake, uncovered, for 20 minutes. Serve immediately, garnished with olives and cherry tomatoes and with additional salsa on the side.

YIELD

8 to 12 6-inch tortillas

Per tortilla
calories 238, protein 5 g,
fat 6 g, sodium 512 mg,
carbohydrates 40 g,
potassium 50 mg

TIME

15 minutes preparation
10 minutes resting
20 to 25 minutes cooking

INGREDIENTS

4 cups unbleached all-purpose flour
2 teaspoons salt
2 teaspoons baking powder
½ teaspoon sugar
4 tablespoons lard
1½ cups warm water

Stir together the dry ingredients, and cut in the lard with a pastry blender ①, or mix with your fingers. Add the water, a little at a time, and work the dough with your hands until it is manageable. Knead dough 15 to 20 times, and let rest for 10 minutes, covered.

Form the dough into balls roughly the size of an egg ② and roll out each with a rolling pin to a circle about 6 inches in diameter and ⅛ inch thick ③.

Meanwhile, set a cast-iron *comal* or griddle over medium heat. Rub it with lard and then wipe it dry with a paper towel. When it is hot, fry the tortillas for about 45 seconds on one side, less on the other, or until small brownish spots appear on the cooked surface. As you bake tortillas, stack in cloth towel. If freezing, package when cooled to prevent sticking.

YIELD

6 burritos

Per burrito
calories 495, protein 18 g,
fat 15 g, sodium 1442 mg,
carbohydrates 73,
potassium 546

TIME

20 minutes preparation
30 minutes cooking

INGREDIENTS

6 Wheat Tortillas (Recipe 13)
2 teaspoons bacon drippings
1 clove garlic, minced
1 can (16 ounces) pinto beans,
    drained
Salt to taste
1/4 cup finely chopped Spanish onions
1/2 cup coarsely chopped monterey
    jack cheese
2 cups coarsely torn romaine lettuce

BURRITO SAUCE

1 tablespoon butter, melted
1 Spanish onion, thinly sliced and
    separated into rings
4 to 6 green chiles, parched, peeled,
    and chopped (see Recipe 21,
    NOTE)
1 clove garlic, minced
1 tablespoon flour
2 medium tomatoes, sliced into
    thin wedges
1 1/2 cups rich chicken broth
1/2 teaspoon salt

Prepare sauce first. Melt butter in a frying pan. Add the onion, chiles, and garlic and cook until onion is transparent. Add the flour and stir; cook until well blended. Add tomatoes. Add the broth and salt and cook until the sauce becomes smooth. Allow to cook about 15 minutes to blend the flavors. Set aside. Makes 1 pint.

If tortillas are not freshly made, cover with aluminum foil and place on dinner plates and warm in a 300-degree oven; otherwise just warm plates. Turn oven to 350 degrees.

Heat drippings, add garlic, and cook until lightly browned, then add the beans, mashing the beans to a pulp ① and seasoning to taste with the salt. Spoon the hot bean mixture down the center of each warm tortilla ②. Top with chopped onions and cheese ③. Roll and heat in the oven until the cheese melts.

Nest chopped lettuce around the warm burritos and serve with a generous supply of Burrito Sauce.

NOTE Chile con Carne (Recipe 23) made from beef or pork can be inserted in the burritos, if desired, but then the cheese and sauce are usually omitted. If preferred, Red Chile Sauce (see Introduction) may be used instead of Burrito Sauce.

BEEF TACOS

YIELD

12 tacos

Per taco (without taco sauce)

calories 234, protein 12 g, fat 12 g, sodium 152 mg, carbohydrates 20 g, potassium 198 mg

TIME

15 minutes preparation
30 minutes cooking

INGREDIENTS

Oil for deep-frying
12 Corn Tortillas (Recipe 7)
   or taco shells
1 pound ground beef
2 tablespoons ground pure red chile
   (mild)
1 tablespoon ground pure red chile
   (hot)
1/2 teaspoon each ground Mexican
   oregano and cumino (cumin)

1 clove garlic, minced
Salt to taste
1 small onion, chopped
2 1/2 cups shredded lettuce
1 fresh tomato, chopped
1 1/2 cups grated cheese
Taco sauce or Salsa Fresca
   (see Introduction)

Heat oil in a deep-fryer or heavy skillet to 375 degrees. Oil should be at least 1 inch deep. Using medium high heat, fry tortillas on both sides ①. Be careful to fry each on one side until slightly crisp but still pliable, then turn using two tongs and fold in half, holding edges of tortillas so as to keep tortilla open enough to hold the filling ②. Allow one side to become crisp, then turn and fry the other side. Drain well, placing a wadded paper towel into each ③. You may want to fry several shells at a time and freeze the additional ones. Keep those you plan to use now warm in a 225-degree oven.

Fry meat until slightly browned, about 5 minutes. Drain excess fat. Add ground chile, oregano, cumino, garlic and salt. Cook another 5 minutes to blend flavors.

Remove tortilla shells from oven and turn temperature to 350 degrees. Place the meat mixture in the warm tortilla shells, then add the chopped onion, 2 cups shredded lettuce, chopped tomato, and the grated cheese. Heat briefly to melt cheese, then serve nested with remaining shredded lettuce. Serve with a side dish of taco sauce or Salsa Fresca. Let guests add the sauce as desired.

YIELD

4 to 6 servings

Per taco (without salsa)
calories 506, protein 28 g,
fat 31 g, sodium 552 mg,
carbohydrates 25 g,
potassium 613 mg

TIME

5 minutes preparation
15 minutes cooking
3 to 4 minutes baking

INGREDIENTS

1½ pounds chicken pieces
½ teaspoon salt
2 teaspoons canning juice from
   jalapeño peppers
12 taco shells
1 clove garlic, crushed
2 cups finely shredded lettuce
1½ cups grated monterey jack cheese

1 large tomato, cut in thin wedges
1 medium avocado, cut in thin slices
Salsa Fresca (see Introduction)

Place chicken in a saucepan, add water to barely cover, and season with salt and jalapeño juice. Bring to a boil, reduce heat, cover, and simmer for 15 minutes.

Turn heat off and let chicken cool completely in the broth. Drain, remove meat from the bones ①, and shred, using 2 forks to do so ②.

Place taco shells in a 225-degree oven to warm. Thoroughly toss crushed garlic clove with shredded lettuce. Remove taco shells from oven and increase temperature to 350 degrees. Assemble tacos by placing into each shell some shredded chicken, some lettuce, and some cheese ③. Return to the oven for 3 or 4 minutes until cheese melts.

Garnish with tomato wedges and avocado slices and serve immediately with a side dish of Salsa Fresca.

YIELD

6 servings

Per serving (without sauce)

calories 1120, protein 44 g,
fat 60 g, sodium 1703 mg,
carbohydrates 98 g,
potassium 1056 mg

TIME

15 minutes preparation
1 hour 15 minutes
cooking

INGREDIENTS

2 pounds stewing beef, coarsely
  chopped
2 cups potatoes, peeled and diced
  small
1 cup hot green chiles, parched and
  peeled (see Recipe 21, NOTE)
2 cloves garlic, minced
1 cup chopped Spanish onion
1½ teaspoons salt
½ teaspoon ground Mexican oregano

¼ teaspoon ground cumino (cumin)
12 Wheat Tortillas (Recipe 13)
Lard for deep-frying
2 cups shredded lettuce
2 ripe tomatoes, cut into wedges
Red Chile Sauce (see Introduction)
1 pint sour cream

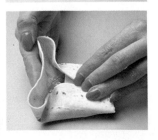

In a skillet or saucepan, place the beef, potatoes, chiles, garlic, onion, salt, oregano, and *cumino*. Add just enough water to cover. Simmer, covered, for at least 1 hour, or until well done and very tender. The mixture should be quite thick; if too "soupy," remove lid and cook until some of the liquid has evaporated. Cool.

Meanwhile, wrap the tortillas in foil and warm them in a 325-degree oven for 15 minutes. Heat about 2 inches of lard to 375 degrees in a heavy skillet.

Divide the filling among the 12 tortillas, placing about 2 heaping tablespoons in the center of each ①. Fold one side of the tortilla over the filling ②, then the 2 adjacent sides, and finally fold the fourth side over ③. Secure with a toothpick.

Fry the filled tortillas until golden, turning to brown evenly. Drain well on paper toweling. Place 2 chimichangos on each of 6 plates and keep them warm in a 250-degree oven until ready to serve. When ready, surround chimichangos on the plates with shredded lettuce and tomato wedges. Spoon Red Chile Sauce on top of each and generous dollops of sour cream in the center.

YIELD

4 to 6 servings

Per serving (4)
calories 526, protein 26 g,
fat 21 g, sodium 222 mg,
carbohydrates 56 g,
potassium 398 mg

TIME

15 minutes preparation
25 minutes cooking

INGREDIENTS

12 Corn Tortillas (Recipe 7)
About 1½ cups cooked meat filling
    such as chile-flavored beef, pork,
    or chicken taco filling
Oil for frying
Chopped lettuce
Taco sauce
Sour cream (optional)

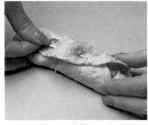

Soften the tortillas, foil-wrapped, in a warm oven for about 15 minutes or by placing each briefly on a hot griddle.

Using 2 spoons, place a narrow pile of filling along the center of each tortilla, working on only one at a time. Roll and secure with a toothpick ①.

While rolling the flautas, heat about ¼ inch oil to medium heat in a large, heavy skillet. Fry each flauta, turning to brown evenly ②. Drain on paper towels ③ and serve garnished with lettuce, taco sauce, and sour cream. Or serve plain, with a bowl of taco sauce or Salsa Fresca (see Introduction) for dipping.

YIELD

24 servings

Per serving (without guacamole)
calories 82, protein 4 g,
fat 5 g, sodium 37 g,
carbohydrates 6 g,
potassium 61 mg

TIME

15 minutes preparation
30 minutes cooking

INGREDIENTS

24 3-inch Corn Tortillas (Recipe 7)
1½ cups, approximately, cooked meat
    filling such as beef, pork, or
    chicken
Lard for frying
Guacamole (see Introduction)

Soften tortillas by placing each briefly on a hot griddle ① or by wrapping in foil ② and heating for 15 minutes in oven.

Working on 1 taquito at a time, place a narrow pile of filling along the center of a tortilla; roll tightly and secure with a wooden pick.

Heat about 1 inch of lard over. medium heat in a large, heavy skillet. Fry the taquitas, turning to brown evenly ③. Drain well on paper toweling and serve with Guacamole.

YIELD

5 to 6 dozen

Per tamale (beef only)
calories 257, protein 4 g,
fat 16 g, sodium 151 mg,
carbohydrates 22 g,
potassium 86 mg

TIME

2 hours preparation
1 hour 30 minutes
    cooking
20 minutes steaming

INGREDIENTS

1½ pounds beef round or lean
    stewing beef, boneless pork, or
    chicken meat
2 tablespoons bacon drippings
2 tablespoons flour
½ cup ground red chile powder
1 teaspoon salt
Pinch of Mexican oregano
1 clove garlic, minced
1½ cups meat stock, approximately
5 to 6 dozen corn husks, rinsed and
    trimmed

TAMALE MASA

6 cups masa harina
3½ cups warm water, approximately
2 cups lard
1½ teaspoons salt

Simmer meat in water to cover over medium to low heat. Cook until tender, about 1 hour. Cut meat into very tiny cubes or chop, using low speed of a food processor or electric blender. Heat the bacon drippings in a large skillet and add the meat. Brown well, then add the flour and, stirring constantly, lightly brown the flour. Remove the pan from the heat; when slightly cooled, add the chile powder and stir. Season with salt, oregano, and garlic. Add a scant cup of meat stock and continue adding more as the mixture simmers, stirring constantly. Cook at least 30 minutes to blend the flavors. The sauce should be very thick and smooth.

Soak the corn husks in warm water until soft. Prepare masa. Add warm water to the masa; allow to stand. Beat the lard, using an electric mixer at medium speed, until quite fluffy and creamy. Add the salt, then combine the lard with the masa, mixing well. Spread each husk with about 2 tablespoons masa ①, then add a strip of meat mixture down the center of the masa. Fold one side of the husk over the masa, covering the meat mixture with the masa ②, then roll the tamale. Fold up the bottom of the husk and tie both ends with strips of corn husk ③. (If planning to freeze the tamales, freeze them at this point and steam them just before serving for best flavor.)

To steam stand upright on a rack in a pressure cooker, deep-fat cooker, or large kettle. Cook under pressure for 20 minutes at 15 pounds pressure, or 45 minutes if steaming with regular heat. (If cooking frozen tamales, increase the cooking time by one half.) Serve with sauce (see Note).

NOTE *To prepare the sauce for topping, use coarser chopped meat and prepare double quantity of filling. After stuffing the tamales, the remaining filling can be thinned for use as a sauce. Or you can substitute Red Chile Sauce (see Introduction).*

YIELD

4 to 6 servings

Per serving (4)
calories 857, protein 35 g,
fat 35 g, sodium 1198 mg,
carbohydrates 100 g,
potassium 263 mg

TIME

30 minutes preparation
5 minutes cooking

INGREDIENTS

12 large green chiles, with stems on,
    parched and peeled (see Note); or
    use 3 cans (4 ounces) whole
    green chiles
8 ounces monterey jack or longhorn
    cheese, cut in long narrow strips
Up to 1 quart vegetable oil

BATTER

1 cup unbleached all-purpose flour
1 teaspoon baking powder
½ teaspoon salt
¾ cup blue cornmeal, or white or
    yellow cornmeal
1 cup milk
2 eggs, slightly beaten

Drain canned chiles between layers of paper toweling; this is important to help the coating stick. Open a small slit below the stem of each chile ①. Insert strips of cheese into each chile, using care not to split the chile ②.

Fifteen minutes before serving, heat either shallow or deep amount of oil to 375 degrees. (Deep fat assures rounder-looking rellenos.) Prepare batter. Combine flour with baking powder and salt, then add cornmeal to flour mixture. Blend milk with eggs, then combine with dry ingredients.

Dip stuffed chiles into batter ③, using a large spoon, tongs, or your hands, and drop into the hot oil. Fry until golden, then drain on absorbent paper towels.

Serve with Red Chile Sauce (see Introduction), or salsa of your choice.

NOTE To remove skins, rinse chiles and drain. Pierce with the sharp point of a knife. If using a gas range, place chiles on an asbestos pad or in a cast-iron skillet to rapidly brown. If using an electric range, place on foil-covered cookie sheet and place about 4 to 6 inches below broiler to rapidly brown. Be sure to turn the chiles as they brown. When browned, place chiles in a cold towel and allow to steam for 10 minutes. Freeze with skins on for greatest ease and versatility; they will come off easily when thawed. If using at once, peel. If used for rellenos, leave stems on. If for stew or in a combination dish, pull stems off and, holding chiles downward, squeeze from the point downward and seeds will squirt out.

YIELD

12 servings

Per serving (without
sour cream)
calories 217, protein 25 g,
fat 11 g, sodium 336 mg,
carbohydrates 3 g,
potassium 485 mg

TIME

15 minutes preparation
2 hours cooking

INGREDIENTS

2 tablespoons lard, butter, or bacon
  drippings
1 large onion, chopped
3 pounds lean beef, in 1-inch cubes
3 cloves garlic, chopped
1 package (.9 ounce) or ¼ cup pure
  ground red chile (hot)
1 package (1 ounce) or ¼ cup pure
  ground red chile (mild) or to taste

1 packet (.8 ounce) or 1½ teaspoons
  ground cumino (cumin) or more to
  taste
3 cups water or more
1½ teaspoons salt

Melt lard in skillet and sauté the onion until soft. Mix the meat with the garlic, chile, and *cumino* ①. Add to the pot ②, along with the water ③. Stir well, adding more water as needed to keep mixture moist. Simmer 2 hours over low heat until the meat is tender and the flavors blended. Add salt to taste after 1 hour. Taste when finished cooking and add more seasonings if desired. If time allows, chill mixture in the refrigerator to allow flavors to mellow. Serve hot. To tame and sophisticate the brew, serve with a dollop of sour cream, a squish of fresh lime, chopped Spanish onion, jalapeño peppers, coarsely grated monterey jack and cheddar cheeses, and squares of lime- and pequín-sprinkled avocado.

NOTE *For a very mild flavor, use only mild chile. For hotter flavor, use all hot chile; and for an even hotter taste, add some caribe and pequín chile as well!*

YIELD

4 to 6 servings

Per serving (4)
calories 748, protein 38 g,
fat 43 g, sodium 1669 mg,
carbohydrates 54 g,
potassium 1496 mg

TIME

5 minutes preparation
45 minutes cooking

INGREDIENTS

1 tablespoon lard
½ cup chopped onion
1 pound ground beef
2 cups tomato sauce
1 clove garlic
1 teaspoon salt
1 tablespoon each ground pure hot
    and mild red chile
½ teaspoon ground cumino (cumin)

¼ teaspoon ground Mexican oregano
2 cups stewed pinto beans (Recipe 4)

Heat lard in a large saucepan, then add the onion and beef ①; cook until meat is lightly browned.

Add tomato sauce ② and simmer for 5 minutes. Add garlic, salt, ground chiles, *cumino*, and oregano; simmer for 30 minutes. Add pinto beans ③ and simmer for 10 more minutes. Taste and adjust seasoning. Ladle chile into soup bowls and serve as suggested for Bowl of Red (Recipe 22).

24

YIELD

4 servings

Per serving (beef only)
calories 338, protein 30 g,
fat 14 g, sodium 680 mg,
carbohydrates 25 g,
potassium 892 mg

TIME

10 minutes preparation
40 minutes cooking

INGREDIENTS

1 pound lean beef or steak, coarsely
  chopped, or good quality lean pork
  roast
1 medium onion, finely chopped
2 large fresh tomatoes, peeled and
  chopped, or 1 cup packed canned
  tomatoes
Pinch of ground cloves
1/4 teaspoon ground cumino (cumin)
1/2 cup seedless raisins, plumped in
  1/4 cup hot beef broth

1 clove garlic, crushed
2 tablespoons vinegar
1 teaspoon sugar
1 teaspoon ground cinnamon
1 teaspoon salt
1/2 cup slivered almonds

Brown the meat in a skillet over medium heat for about 5 minutes ①. After meat begins to cook and some of the fat begins to cook out, add the onion. Cook until onion is translucent, about 5 more minutes. Drain off excess fat, if any ②.

Add all remaining ingredients except almonds ③. Simmer for about 30 minutes. Add the almonds just before serving; use them as a garnish for the top of the dish.

YIELD

6 servings

Per serving
calories 446, protein 41 g,
fat 23 g, sodium 1197 mg,
carbohydrates 18 g,
potassium 802 mg

TIME

30 minutes preparation
1½ hours cooking

INGREDIENTS

1 roasting chicken about 4 pounds,
  cut up
Celery tops
1 carrot, quartered
1 medium Spanish onion, half
  quartered and half chopped
2 teaspoons salt
1 slice dry bread
2 tablespoons seedless raisins
½ ounce (½ square) unsweetened
  chocolate

¼ cup blanched almonds
1 cup finely chopped green pepper
2 cups quartered fresh tomato
1 garlic clove, minced
3 tablespoons flour
¼ teaspoon ground cinnamon
1 tablespoon ground pure hot red
  chile
¼ teaspoon ground cloves
2½ cups chicken broth

Place chicken in a pot, add cold water to barely cover. Add celery tops, carrot, quartered half onion, and salt. Cover and cook until tender, about 1 hour. Set aside and cool.

Using a food processor, electric blender, or mortar and pestle, grind chopped onion, bread, raisins, chocolate, almonds, green pepper, tomato, and garlic ①. Stir in flour and spices, then add chicken broth and mix until well blended ②.

Cook sauce until slightly thickened. Taste and adjust seasonings. Add chicken pieces ③ and simmer gently for 30 minutes, basting frequently. Serve with steamed rice. Leftovers are wonderful for filling tacos, omelettes, or tamales.

YIELD

4 servings

Per serving
calories 1023, protein 35 g,
fat 93 g, sodium 1152 mg,
carbohydrates 10 g,
potassium 886 mg

TIME

5 minutes preparation
3 hours marinating
2 hours baking

INGREDIENTS

2 pounds lean pork spareribs
6 cloves garlic, minced
1 teaspoon salt
¼ cup olive oil
Freshly ground black pepper
¼ cup red wine vinegar
½ teaspoon Mexican oregano
¼ cup minced onion
1 can (8 ounces) tomato sauce
1 cup Red Chile Sauce (see
    Introduction)

Slice ribs into individual portions ① and place in oblong baking pan. Sprinkle with garlic, salt, oil, pepper, vinegar, oregano, and onion ②. Let stand for about 3 hours at room temperature.

Preheat oven to 350 degrees. Mix tomato sauce and chile sauce together and pour over the ribs ③. Place in oven and bake for 2 hours.

NOTE If in a hurry, the mixed tomato and chile sauce may be added after only 15 minutes of marinating. You can freeze up to 3 months, baked or unbaked.

YIELD

4 to 6 servings

Per serving (4)
calories 555, protein 39 g,
fat 22 g, sodium 891 mg,
carbohydrates 47 g,
potassium 681 mg

TIME

5 minutes preparation
30 minutes marinating
5 minutes cooking

INGREDIENTS

1½ pounds very lean, well-trimmed
  round steak, cut into ½-inch-thick
  slices about 6 inches long and 3 to
  4 inches wide (known regionally as
  skirt steaks)
Juice of ½ lime
4 large cloves garlic, minced
½ teaspoon or more kosher salt
Freshly ground black pepper to taste
4 to 6 12-inch Wheat Tortillas
  (Recipe 13)

4 to 6 leaves romaine or curly red leaf
  lettuce
Guacamole (see Introduction)
Salsa Fresca (see Introduction) or good
  quality purchased salsa
¼ cup chopped Spanish onion
1 medium tomato, chopped
½ cup coarsely chopped fresh cilantro
½ pint sour cream

Prepare skirt steaks by closely trimming all fat and sinew. Pound to flatten and tenderize ①. In a medium bowl, just large enough in diameter to hold steaks, place lime juice. Put a steak in bowl, pressing into the lime juice ②. Sprinkle with garlic, salt, and pepper. Push to side and repeat until all steaks are covered ③, stacking all together. Put bowl aside to marinate, 30 minutes. Turn once or twice during marination.

Place 4 to 6 serving plates in warm (250-degree) oven, with tortillas wrapped in foil. Rinse lettuce and drain. Heat large, heavy, well-seasoned frying pan on high heat. Lightly oil surface. When a drop of moisture "dances" on the surface, add steak pieces. Quickly cook each side about 2 to 2½ minutes.

To serve, divide the meat among the number of plates, placing it directly atop a tortilla. Allow guests to top steak as they desire with the lettuce, guacamole, salsa, onion, tomato, cilantro, and sour cream; or serve the steaks already sauced and garnished. Roll, folding the bottom over the filling first, then folding each side over and rolling together. Serve with added salsa.

NOTE Traditionally, these steaks are grilled over mesquite and served with Pico de Gallo (cock's comb)—the hot, hot jalapeño-flavored sauce made from chipotles (smoked jalapeños) and freshly cooked beans, sometimes with sour cream. The above version is for Northerners—out of fresh jalapeños, chipotles, mesquite, and freshly cooked pintos—but it is guaranteed to please hungry hands!! You may wish to serve tostadas to dip into guacamole and salsa.

YIELD

5 dozen

Per cookie

calories 137, protein 1 g,
fat 8 g, sodium 55 mg,
carbohydrates 15 g,
potassium 15 mg

TIME

15 minutes preparation
10 minutes baking

INGREDIENTS

6 cups sifted all-purpose flour
2½ teaspoons baking powder
1 teaspoon salt
1 pound lard
1¾ cups sugar
2 teaspoons anise seed
2 eggs
¼ cup brandy, approximately, or
    sherry or apple cider
1 tablespoon cinnamon

Preheat oven to 350 degrees.

Sift flour with baking powder and salt. Whip lard until fluffy; add 1½ cups sugar slowly ①. Mix in anise seed.

Beat eggs until light and fluffy; add to the creamed mixture ②. Add flour mixture and brandy and mix until well blended. Use only enough brandy to form a stiff dough.

Knead slightly and pat or roll to ¼ inch to ½ inch thick ③ and cut into fancy shapes. The *fleur de lis* shape is traditional for these cookies. Make it by cutting the dough into diamonds, then combine remaining sugar and cinnamon and dust top of each cookie in a mixture of sugar and cinnamon. Bake 10 minutes or until very lightly browned.

YIELD

4 to 6 servings

Per serving (4)
calories 162, protein 5 g,
sodium 41 mg,
carbohydrates 31 g,
potassium 234 mg

TIME

10 to 15 minutes
  preparation
15 minutes chilling

INGREDIENTS

1.½ cups chilled fresh-squeezed
  orange juice, made from 3 large
  oranges, or ½ cup pulpy orange
  concentrate mixed with 1 cup iced
  water with crushed ice
1 envelope unflavored gelatin
¼ cup boiling water
¼ cup Triple Sec or Cointreau
2 tablespoons wild Seville orange
  marmalade or regular marmalade

3 egg whites
3 tablespoons sugar
Bittersweet chocolate curls or
  chocolate candies, crumbled
  (optional)

Place chilled orange juice in a 1-quart mixing bowl.

Sprinkle gelatin over boiling water and stir until dissolved ①. Add to orange juice. Add Triple Sec and 1 tablespoon marmalade. Blend together well. Place in freezer for about 10 to 15 minutes.

Meanwhile, beat egg whites to soft peaks ②. Sprinkle 1 tablespoon sugar over the top and continue to beat, adding remaining 2 tablespoons, beating after each addition until stiff peaks form.

When orange mixture is syrupy (somewhat thickened), carefully fold in the egg whites, using an up and over motion ③. When well combined, place in 4 large, or 6 medium, stemmed goblets or sherbet glasses. To serve, top each with some remaining marmalade and chocolate curls or crumbled candies.

INDEX

MAIL ORDER SOURCES FOR MEXICAN INGREDIENTS

Adobe House
127 Payne Street
Dallas, Texas 75207

Ashley's Mexican Foods
Division Bruce Foods Corp.
P.O. Drawer 1030
New Iberia, Louisiana 70560

Casados Farms/Dos Ves, Inc.
Box 1269
San Juan Pueblo, New Mexico
87566

Casa Moneo
210 West 14th Street
New York, New York 10011

El Molino Tamales
117 So. 22nd Street
Phoenix, Arizona 85034

H. Roth and Son
1577 First Avenue
New York, New York 10021

Jane Butel's Pecos Valley
   Spice Co.
142 Lincoln Avenue
Santa Fe, New Mexico 87051

La Semillera Horticultural
   Enterprises
P.O. Box 34082
Dallas, Texas 75234

Sasabe Store
   "Hot Stuff"
P.O. Box 7
Sasabe, Arizona 85704

Simon David Grocery Store
7117 Inwood Road
Dallas, Texas 78207

Taos Chili Company
Turley Mill Building
Box 1100 B.A.
Taos, New Mexico 87571

Tia Mia
Dept. BA 03
Sunland Park, New Mexico
88063